6/18 LG BL:0.8 AR:0.5

TOOLS FOR TEACHERS

- **ATOS:** 0.8
- **GRL:** E
- **LEXILE:** 210L
- **CURRICULUM CONNECTIONS:** animals
- **WORD COUNT:** 71

Skills to Teach

- **HIGH-FREQUENCY WORDS:** a, but, he, him, his, in, is, it, jumps, play, runs, the
- **CONTENT WORDS:** barn, clean, foal, grazes, hungry, legs, mother, nurses, outside, spring, tired
- **PUNCTUATION:** periods, comma
- **WORD STUDY:** long /o/, spelled oa (*foal*); r-controlled vowels (*barn, mother, nurses*); consonant cluster cks (*licks*); initial s-blends sm (*small*), st (*stands*), spr (*spring*), str (*stretches*)
- **TEXT TYPE:** factual recount

Before Reading Activities

- Read the title and give a simple statement of the main idea.
- Have students "walk" though the book and talk about what they see in the pictures.
- Introduce new vocabulary by having students predict the first letter and locate the word in the text.
- Discuss any unfamiliar concepts that are in the text.

After Reading Activities

Encourage children to talk about the different things a foal is shown doing in the book. List the different behaviors, such as nursing, running, and jumping, on the board and consider which farm babies (piglets, chicks, calves, etc.) might do the same things. Would a calf nurse? How about a chick? Following their suggestions, write the animal's name underneath the behavior.

Tadpole Books are published by Jump!, 5357 Penn Avenue South, Minneapolis, MN 55419, www.jumplibrary.com

Editor: Jenny Fretland VanVoorst **Designer:** Anna Peterson

Photo Credits: Alamy: Sorge, 4–5; Slawik, C./juniors@wildlife, 8–9. Dreamstime: Rkpimages, 10–11. Getty: Life on White, cover. Shutterstock: Eric Isselee, 1; MaxyM, 2–3; Steve Heap, 2–3; purplequeue, 6–7; mkant, 12–13; rokopix, 14–15.

Library of Congress Cataloging-in-Publication Data
Names: Mayerling, Tim.
Title: Foals / by Tim Mayerling.
Description: Minneapolis, Minnesota: Jump!, Inc., 2017. | Series: Farm babies | Audience: Age 3–6. | Includes index.
Identifiers: LCCN 2017004271 (print) | LCCN 2017009094 (ebook) | ISBN 9781620317679 (hardcover: alk. paper) | ISBN 9781620317877 (pbk.) | ISBN 9781624966149 (ebook)
Subjects: LCSH: Foals—Juvenile literature. | Foals—Pictorial works—Juvenile literature. | Horses—Juvenile literature | Horses—Pictorial works—Juvenile literature.
Classification: LCC SF302 .M2495 2017 (print) | LCC SF302 (ebook) | DDC 636.1/07—dc23
LC record available at https://lccn.loc.gov/2017004271LC record available at https://lccn.loc.gov/2016058409

FARM BABIES

FOALS

by Tim Mayerling

TABLE OF CONTENTS

tadpole
books

FOALS

It is spring.

barn

In the barn, a foal is born.

foal

He is small.
He is wet.

His mother licks him.
Now he is clean.

**The foal stands.
He is wobbly.**

He is hungry.
He nurses.

The barn is warm.
It is safe.

But the foal wants to play.

He goes outside.

He runs.

He jumps.

He stretches his legs.

**Now he is tired.
He lies down.**

His mother
grazes nearby.

WORDS TO KNOW

barn

jump

lick

nurse

run

spring

INDEX